The Amazing Incredible Shrinking Ukulele

Story by Thornton Cline
Illustrations by Susan Oliver

ISBN: 978-1-57424-335-2
SAN 683-8022

Cover by James Creative Group

All Illustrations by Susan Oliver

"This well-told story with a good moral is certainly one young readers can relate to. Delightful illustrations add to the fun and help make this whimsical book come alive."
– *Dick Sheridan, Best Selling Ukulele Book Author*

"A great illustration on the importance of musical creativity, persistence, encouragement, and having an artistic outlet for children. When my son was five, we told him he had to play an instrument for one year and that he was required, like with any class in school, to apply himself. If he didn't want to continue after a year, he could quit. He is now 22. We tour full time as a father/son duo. Guitar, Fiddle, Mandolin, and Vocals."

– *Tim Thompson, 2008 Fingerstyle Champion & Full Time Touring Guitarist, Singer Songwriter & Producer Timandmyles.com*

The Amazing Shrinking Incredible Ukulele

Trevor was a fifth grader who tried to be as cool as the coolest kid in his class.

After school one day his mom said, "Your dad and I think you should learn to play a musical instrument."

"No, Mom, I'm too busy."

"You'd have fun," his mom said. "Close your eyes. I have a surprise."

Trevor opened his eyes to discover a strange-looking case.

"What's this, Mom?"

"Open it," she said. "Your dad and I bought this nice ukulele in a music store. And we found a good teacher. His name is Mr. Parker."

"Mom, I'm not really interested in the ukulele," said Trevor.

He let out a big yawn and left the room without saying anything.

"You're welcome," his mom shouted.

At dinner, Trevor's dad asked, "Did you like the ukulele?"

Trevor didn't answer.

"Did you like the ukulele?" his Dad asked again.

"Why didn't you get me a cooler instrument something like an electric guitar?" he asked.

"This was a gift, Son. You should be grateful."

Trevor got up from the table and went into his room.

All week his new ukulele sat untouched in the closet of his room.

On Saturday morning at breakfast, his mom said, "Your first lesson is today."

"Mom, do I really have to go?"

"At least give it a chance," said his mom.

Trevor decided it was easier to go than to hear his mom bug him.

Trevor met his new ukulele teacher. Mr. Parker tried to teach him, but Trevor wasn't interested. He strummed a few chords just to please Mr. Parker.

"If this is how you're going to act when you come to lessons, you might want rethink about coming back," he told Trevor.

"Okay, I'll think about it," Trevor replied.

For weeks Trevor didn't practice and didn't try in his lessons. He didn't have his heart into it. Mr. Parker and Trevor's parents worked hard to get Trevor interested in his ukulele.

One night when Trevor was asleep, a strange-looking man dressed like a rock star suddenly woke him.

"Who are you?" Trevor asked in a startled way.

"Don't you know who I am?"

"Are you a ghost?" Trevor asked.

"You could say that, kid. But don't be afraid, I'm not here to hurt you."

"I was a former ukulele and guitar rock star."

Trevor pulled the covers up to his eyes and stared nervously at him.

"I used to have an attitude like yours," he said. "I wanted to play the electric guitar because it was cool. But my mom gave me ukulele lessons instead. I tried to quit, but the more I played, the more I loved it. I got so good on both instruments that later on I became a famous rock star."

"You were a famous rock star?"

"You could say that!" said the man.

"Why are you here?" Trevor asked.

"I came to warn you and help you," he said. "If you quit playing the ukulele and stop your lessons, your ukulele will shrink until it vanishes."

"So what, I'm not very good at it."

"There you go, your attitude is showing," he said.

Trevor pulled the covers over his head.

"Not only will your ukulele shrink, you'll regret it. If you're thinking of playing the electric guitar too, you don't have a ghost of a chance," he said.

"Seriously?" Trevor asked as he pulled the covers from his face.

"Yes, seriously," the man said as he faded into the dark.

Trevor thought it was a dream and went back to sleep.

The next day he totally forgot about it.

Weeks passed. He continued to give half of his heart to practicing and his lessons.

One Saturday afternoon as Trevor was leaving his house for lessons, he noticed his ukulele case felt lighter than usual. But he paid no attention to it.

At his lesson, Trevor opened his case. His eyes grew wide with surprise. His ukulele had shrunk to the size of a harmonica. He was too embarrassed to show Mr. Parker. He stuffed his tiny ukulele into his jeans pocket.

"I left my ukulele at home," he said.

"How could you do that?"

Trevor didn't answer. He closed his ukulele case.

"I'll be sure to let your mom and dad know about it and we'll reschedule a lesson," Mr. Parker said.

As Trevor waited for his parents to pick him up he thought about what the ghost rock star had said. And yes his ukulele had shrunk to the size of a harmonica.

Day after day, he tried to play his small ukulele. It was difficult to get his fingers to play the chords or notes due to its tiny size. But Trevor kept trying hard and his attitude changed. His ukulele gradually grew back to its original size.

Weeks passed and Trevor sounded really good on his ukulele. He was proud of himself. He even enjoyed playing it. "You have improved so much!" said his parents.

"Trevor, you're doing so well. Keep up the good work. I'm proud of you!" Mr. Parker said.

"You sound so good on the ukulele that one day I'll sign you up for guitar lessons as well. You can play both just like famous rock stars today," his mom said.

Trevor flashed a great big proud smile.

"I guess the man was right," said Trevor. "You've got to really try and give it your very best, even if you don't think you'll like it. And maybe I'll become a famous rock star too!"

THE END.

Song Titles

Give It A Try

Thornton Cline

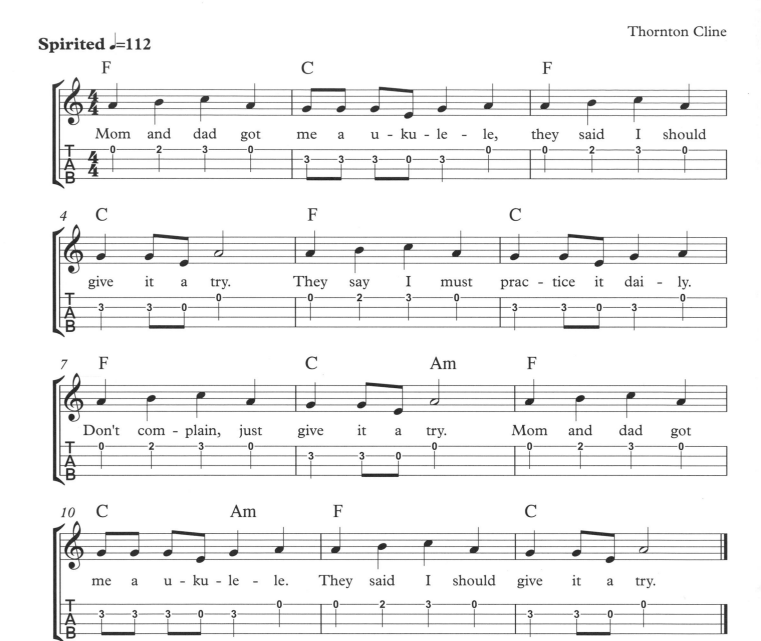

I Love Ukulele

Thornton Cline

Big Rock Star

Thornton Cline

Cheerful ♩=112

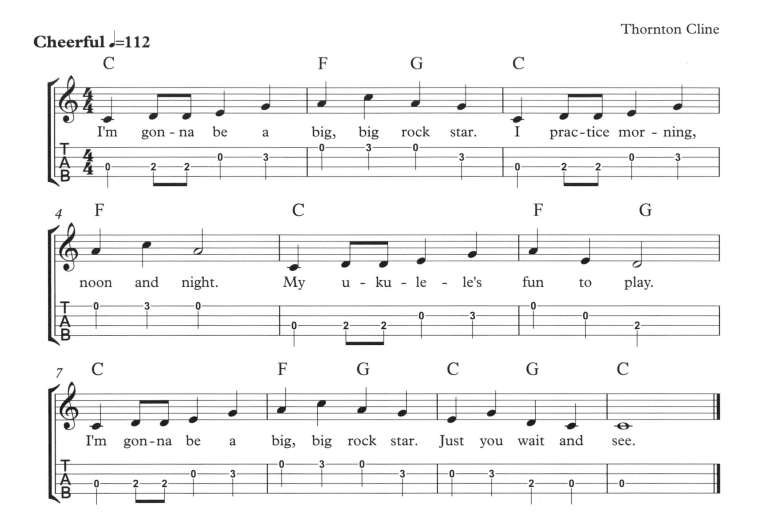

I'm gon-na be a big, big rock star. I prac-tice mor-ning,
noon and night. My u-ku-le-le's fun to play.
I'm gon-na be a big, big rock star. Just you wait and see.

36

I'm Proud of You

I'm Trying

Thornton Cline

Don't You Know Who I Am?

Thornton Cline

My First Lesson

Thornton Cline

Moody ♩=96

My first les - son is to - day. I'm not sure I

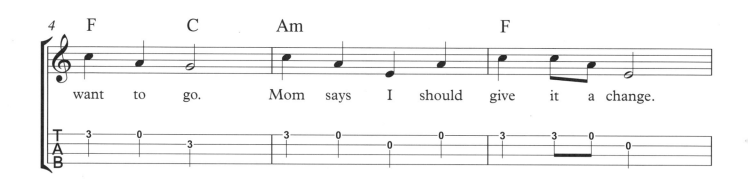

want to go. Mom says I should give it a change.

She says I'll rea-lly like my__ tea-cher. I could be real-ly good on the u-ku-le-le.

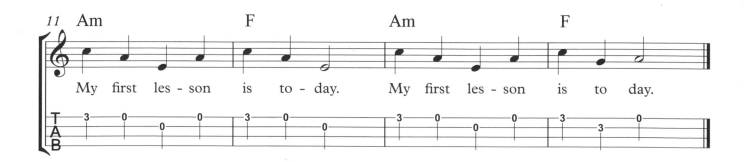

My first les - son is to - day. My first les - son is to day.

I Didn't Quit

Thornton Cline

My Ukulele Is Shrinking

Thornton Cline

42

My Ukulele Is Growing

Thornton Cline

Biographies

Thornton Cline is author of eleven books: *Band of Angels, Practice Personalities: What's Your Type? Practice Personalities for Adults, The Contrary, The Amazing Incredible Shrinking Violin, The Amazing Incredible Shrinking Piano, The Amazing Incredible Shrinking Guitar, The Amazing Musical Magical Plants, A Travesty of Justice, Not My Time to Go,* and Cline's fifth children's book, *The Amazing Incredible Shrinking Ukulele.* Thornton Cline has been honored with "Songwriter of the Year" twice in a row by the Tennessee Songwriter's Association for his hit song, "Love is the Reason," recorded by Engelbert Humperdinck and Gloria Gaynor. Cline has received Dove and Grammy Award nominations for his songs. Thornton Cline is an in-demand author, teacher, speaker, clinician, performer and songwriter. He lives in Hendersonville, Tennessee with his wife, Audrey.

Susan Oliver is an award-winning songwriter and visual artist as well as illustrator. She is originally from Orono, Maine and attended the University of Maine as well as Portland School of Art. Known for her wide variety of styles, Susan has exhibited her artwork and also worked as a graphic designer. Her painting, "Moonlight Seals" gained national attention in efforts to raise funds for Marine Animal Lifeline, an organization dedicated to seal rescue and rehabilitation. Susan now resides outside of Nashville, Tennessee where she continues to write music and design art work for album covers for various musical artists, as well as illustrates children's books. *The Amazing Incredible Shrinking Ukulele* is Oliver's fifth children's book published as an illustrator.

Credits

Audrey

Alex Cline

Mollie Cline

God

Ron Middlebrook

Susan Oliver

Centerstream/Hal Leonard

Crystal Bowman

Sumner Academy

Cumberland Arts Academy

Cumberland University

Jonathan Edwards Classical Academy

Hendersonville Christian Academy

Clinetel Music

Gallatin Creative Arts Center

Lawrence Boothby, photographer

Another Amazing Book!

THE AMAZING MAGICAL MUSICAL PLANTS

Story by Thornton Cline & Crystal Bowman, Illustrations by Susan Oliver

Mr. Jones is having trouble motivating his fifth grade band students to practice. When he discovers a packet of magical musical plant seeds in an old trombone case, he gets an idea. Mr. Jones plants the seeds in pots of soil and gives one to each of his students to take home. He tells the students how to care for the seeds and to play their instruments every day to make the plants grow. Some of his students laugh at his crazy idea, but some of his students take him seriously. The whimsical illustrations by acclaimed illustrator Susan Oliver add to the charm of this delightful story. The book includes a CD of ten easy original songs with recorded examples of each instrument. (Recommended for ages 4-8)

00155787 Book/CD Pack..$19.99

CENTERSTREAM®

P.O. Box 17878 - Anaheim Hills, CA 92817
(714) 779-9390   www.centerstream-usa.com

More Amazing Books!

THE AMAZING INCREDIBLE SHRINKING VIOLIN

Story by Thornton Cline, Illustrations by Susan Oliver

Young Austin begs his parents to play violin. But Austin doesn't make time to practice until one night he is visited by the violin fairy who warns him that if he doesn't practice his violin, it will shrink. Austin's classmates are amazed at what happens next! Austin discovers that if he wants to sound good, he must practice. This heartwarming story teaches the benefits of hard work and attaining one's goals. Austin's dream of becoming a big violin star is starting to come true. The book's whimsical illustrations by acclaimed illustrator Susan Oliver add to the charm and merriment of the story. The book includes a CD of 10 easy original songs for violin or voice (with lyrics sung by a children's choir) and narrations of the story. (Recommended for ages 4-8)

00142509 Book/CD Pack.................................$19.99

THE AMAZING INCREDIBLE SHRINKING PIANO

Story by Thornton Cline, Illustrations by Susan Oliver

Lily is given a piano from her grandmother for her birthday. Lily continues to slam her hands against the keys with anger when she makes mistakes. One night she is visited by her grandmother in a dream who warns Lily not to hit her piano anymore or it will shrink. Lily discovers the secret of how to keep her piano from shrinking. This heartwarming story teaches the respect of the piano. Lily learns how to play beautiful music on her piano without hitting her piano keys. The whimsical illustrations by acclaimed illustrator Susan Oliver add to the charm and merriment of the story. The book includes a CD of 10 easy original songs for piano or voice (with lyrics sung by a children's choir) and narrations of the story. (Recommended for ages 4-8)

00149098 Book/CD Pack.................................$19.99

P.O. Box 17878 - Anaheim Hills, CA 92817

(714) 779-9390   www.centerstream-usa.com

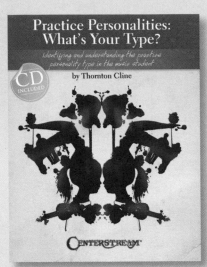